D1515761

Heart to Heart
Copyright 2000 by the Zondervan Corporation
ISBN 0-310-98100-X

All Scripture quotations unless otherwise noted, are taken from the *Holy Bible, New International Version*® (North American Edition). Copyright 1973, 1978, 1984, by International Bible Society. Used by permission of ZondervanPublishingHouse. All rights reserved.

The "NIV" and "New International Version" trademarks are registered in the United States Patent and Trademark Office by International Bible Society.

All rights reserved. No part of this publication may be reproduced, stored in a retrieval system, or transmitted in any form or by any means—electronic, mechanical, photocopy, recording, or any other—except for brief quotations in printed reviews, without the prior permission of the publisher.

Requests for information should be addressed to:
ZondervanPublishingHouse
Grand Rapids, Michigan 49530
http://www.zondervan.com

Project Editor: Molly C. Detweiler
Creative Director: Patricia Matthews
Photography: Photographic Concepts
Design: Veldheer Creative Services

Printed in China

00 01 02 03 /HK/ 5 4 3 2

To:

_____

From:

_____

I have you in my heart.

Philippians 1:7

How precious to me are your thoughts, O God!
How vast is the sum of them!

Were I to count them,
they would outnumber the grains of sand.

Psalm 139:17–18

Grains of Sand

How many grains of sand on the beach?
How many blades of grass in the meadow?
How many drops of dew on the tree?
If you could count all these,
You could count the number of God's blessings.

Praise be to the God and Father of our
Lord Jesus Christ, who has blessed us with
every spiritual blessing in Christ.

Ephesians 1:3

Scatter your seeds of kindness
All enriching as you go—
Leave them. Trust the Harvest Giver;
He will make each seed grow.
So until the happy end
Your life shall never lack a friend.

Sing to the LORD with thanksgiving.
He covers the sky with clouds;
he supplies the earth with rain
and makes grass grow on the hills.

Psalm 147:7–8

Hold fast to your dreams!

Within your heart
Keep one still, secret spot
Where dreams may go,
And sheltered so,
May thrive and grow
Where doubt and fear are not;
O keep a place apart
Within your heart
For little dreams to go!

Louise Driscoll

Best of All

These are the things I prize
And hold of dearest worth:
Light of the sapphire skies,
Peace of the silent hills,
Shelter of the forest, comfort of the grass,
Music of the birds, murmur of the little rills,
Shadows of the clouds that swiftly pass,
And, after showers,
The smell of flowers
And of the good brown earth—
And best of all, along the way, friendship and mirth.

Henry Van Dyke

Your love has given me great
joy and encouragement.

Philemon 7

He prayeth well who loveth well
Both man and bird and beast;
He prayeth best who loveth best
All things both great and small;
For the dear God who loveth us,
He made and loveth all.

Samuel Taylor Coleridge

To love abundantly is to live
abundantly, and to love forever
is to live forever.

No love, no friendship can cross
the path of our destiny without
leaving some mark on it forever.

Francois Mauriac

A good deed is never lost; he
who sows courtesy reaps
friendship, and he who plants
kindness gathers love.

St. Basil

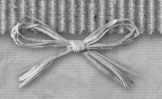

Give love, and love to your life will flow,
A strength in your utmost need;
Have faith, and a score of hearts will show
Their faith in your word and deed.
Give truth and your gift will be paid in kind,
And honor will honor meet;
And a smile that is sweet will surely find
A smile that is just as sweet.

Madeline Bridges

Jesus said, "Again, I tell you that if two of you on earth
agree about anything you ask for, it will be done for
you by my Father in heaven. For where two or three
come together in my name, there am I with them."

Matthew 18:19–20

Drop a word of cheer and kindness:
just a flash and it is gone;
But there's half-a-hundred ripples
circling on and on,
Bearing hope and joy and comfort on
each splashing, dashing wave.
Till you wouldn't believe the volume
of the one kind word you gave.

James W. Foley

The river of Thy grace is flowing free,
We launch upon its depths to sail to Thee;

In the ocean of Thy love we soon shall be,
We are sailing to eternity.

Paul Rader

Like a house without a dooryard,
Like a yard without a flower,
Like a clock without a mainspring,
That will never tell the hour;
A thing that sort of makes you feel
A hunger all the while—
Oh the saddest sight that ever was
Is a face without a smile!

So smile and don't forget to smile,
And smile and smile again;
'Twill help you all along the way,
And cheer you mile by mile;
And so, whatever is your lot,
Just smile and smile and smile.

A Friend's Greeting

I'd like to be the sort of friend that
you have been to me
I'd like to be the help that you've
always been glad to be;
I'd like to mean as much to you each
minute of the day
As you have meant, old friend of
mine, to me along the way.

Edgar A. Guest

Grace and peace to you from God
our Father and from the Lord Jesus
Christ.... I thank my God through
Jesus Christ for all of you.

Romans 1:7–8

Symphony

There is no music so gentle,
No sound so sweet,
No praise so pleasant
As the praise, sound and music
Of that simple word "Love."
The word itself is like a song,
Let's dance, sing and play.
The symphony of love.

The Miracle of Friendship

There's a miracle called friendship
That dwells within the heart,
And you don't know how it happens
Or where it gets its start.
But the happiness it brings you
Always gives a special lift,
And you realize that friendship
Is life's most precious gift.

I love you,
Not only for what you are,
But for what I am
when I am with you.

I love you,
Not only for what
You have made of yourself,
But for what you are making of me.

You have done it
Without a touch
Without a word
Without a sign.
You have done it
By being yourself.
Perhaps that is what
Being a friend means,
after all.

Roy Croft

Dear friends, since God so loved us,
we also ought to love one another.

1 John 4:11

O LORD, how sweet are your words to my taste, sweeter than honey to my mouth!

Psalm 119:103

There comes to my heart one sweet strain,
A glad and a joyous refrain,
I sing it again and again,
Sweet peace, the gift of God's love.
Peace, peace, sweet peace,
Wonderful peace from above,
Oh, wonderful, wonderful peace,
Sweet peace, the gift of God's love.

Peter Philip Bilhorn

The love we give away is the only love we keep.

Elbert Hubbard

Folk want a lot of loving every minute—
The sympathy of others and their smile!
Till life's end, from the moment they begin it,
Folks need a lot of loving all the while.

Strickland Gillian

To be happy is not to possess much,
but to hope and to love much.

Felicité Robert de Lamennais

Flowers are lovely; love is flower-like;
Friendship is a sheltering tree;
Oh the joys that came down shower-like,
Of friendship, love, and liberty.

Samuel Taylor Coleridge

Dear friend, I pray that you may enjoy good
health and that all may go well with you.

3 John 1:2

When the curtains of night are pinned back by stars,
And the beautiful moon leaps in the skies,
And the dewdrops of heaven are kissing the rose,
It is then that my memory flies
As if on the wings of some beautiful dove
In haste with the message it bears
To bring you a kiss of affection and say:
I'll remember you, love, in my prayers.

I always thank my God as I remember you in my prayers.

Philemon 4

Love is life's end (an end, but neverending)
All joys, all sweets, all happiness awarding.

For love is but the heart's immortal thirst
To be completely known and all forgiven.

Henry Van Dyke

Love is never lost. If not reciprocated, it will flow
back and soften and purify the heart.

Washington Irving

The spectrum of love has eight
ingredients: patience, kindness,
generosity, courtesy, unselfishness,
good temper, honesty, and sincerity.

Henry Drummond

I'd like to do the big things and the
splendid things for you,
To brush the gray from out your skies
and leave them only blue
I'd like to say the kindly things
I so oft have heard,
And feel that I could rouse your soul
the way that mine you've stirred.

Edgar A. Guest

The pleasantness of one's friend
springs from his earnest counsel.

Proverbs 27:9

Pleasant words are a honeycomb,
sweet to the soul and healing to the bones.

Proverbs 16:24

Do everything in love.

1 Corinthians 16:14

Some of us know what it is to love,
and we know that could we only
have our way, our beloved ones
would be overwhelmed with
blessings. All that is good, and
sweet, and lovely in life would be
poured out upon them from our
lavish hands, had we but the power
to carry out our will for them.
And if this is the way of love with us,
how much more must it be so with
our God, who is love itself.

Hannah Whitall Smith

It's Up To You

One smile begins a friendship,
One handclasp lifts a soul.
One star can guide a ship at sea,
One word can frame the goal.

One step must start the journey,
One word must start each prayer.
One hope will raise our spirits,
One touch can show you care.

One voice can speak with wisdom,
One heart can know what's true.
One life can make the difference,
You see, its up to you.

Let the rivers clap their hands,
let the mountains sing together for joy;
let them sing before the LORD.

Psalm 98:8–9

The sunshine is brighter
My cares seem much lighter
The stream is more bubbly
And the flowers more lovely
When I share them with you, dear friend!

The thread of life would be dark,
Heaven knows!

If it were not with friendship
and love intertwin'd.

Thomas Moore

Friends are those people who know the words to
the song in your heart and sing them back to you
when you have forgotten the words.

A faithful friend is a strong defense;
And he that hath found him hath found a treasure.

Louisa May Alcott

Sing to the LORD a new song,
for he has done marvelous things.

Psalm 98:1

Grace, mercy and peace from God the Father
and from Jesus Christ, the Father's Son, will be
with us in truth and love.

2 John 3